QUILT SAVVY

Fallert's Guide to Images on Fabric

To Brenda
Happy Printing
Caryl Bryer Fallert

CARYL BRYER FALLERT

American Quilter's Society
P. O. Box 3290 • Paducah, KY 42002-3290
www.americanquilter.com

QUILT SAVVY

Fallert's Guide to Images on Fabric

CARYL BRYER FALLERT

 American Quilter's Society
P. O. Box 3290 • Paducah, KY 42002-3290
www.americanquilter.com

Located in Paducah, Kentucky, the American Quilter's Society (AQS) is dedicated to promoting the accomplishments of today's quilters. Through its publications and events, AQS strives to honor today's quiltmakers and their work and to inspire future creativity and innovation in quiltmaking.

EDITOR: TONI TOOMEY
GRAPHIC DESIGN: LYNDA SMITH
COVER DESIGN: MICHAEL BUCKINGHAM
PHOTOGRAPHY: CARYL BRYER FALLERT,
          CHARLES R. LYNCH

Library of Congress Cataloging-in-Publication Data
  Fallert, Caryl Bryer
    Quilt Savvy: Fallert's Guide to Images on Fabric / by Caryl Bryer Fallert
      p. cm.
    ISBN 1-57432-842-5

Additional copies of this book may be ordered from the American Quilter's Society, PO Box 3290, Paducah, KY 42002-3290; 800-626-5420 (orders only please); or online at www.americanquilter.com. For all other inquiries, call 270-898-7903.

RIGHT: Detail, KORUNDA, by the author. Full quilt pictured on pages 114–115.

DEDICATED

To all the enthusiastic and creative "over 50" quilters who have the courage to learn not only new sewing and design skills, but a whole new world of digital technology. I feel privileged to be among you.

And to the "under 30" crowd, who keep us stretching our brains and our creativity with new tools for self-expression.

ABOVE : Detail, STARS OF AFRICA.
Full quilt pictured on pages 16–17.
LEFT: Detail, OSWEGO AUTUMN #1, by the author.
Full quilt pictured on pages 112–113.

THANK YOU

To Jerome Jenkins for inventing Bubble Jet Set and for taking the time to help quilters with endless technical questions.

To Hewlett Packard for making wonderful printers and for supporting the quilters who use them.

To Jan Cabral and Judy Levine for tutoring me in the computer basics.

And to Terri, Cathy, Maria, Beth, Aileen, Roberta, and Sharon, whose help at the Bryerpatch Studio has allowed me to continue to pursue my Muse.

RIGHT: *Detail, CHRISTINE'S GARDEN, by the author. Full quilt pictured on pages 88–89.*

CONTENTS

LEFT: Detail, SPLENDOR IN THE GRASS, by the author. Full quilt pictured on pages 52–53.

INTRODUCTION

For many years, I have been interested in incorporating photos and images printed from my computer into my quilts. My experiments included photo silk screen, photocopying, and transfer sheets, as well as several formulas that were supposed to set color inkjet printer ink. Unfortunately, none of these methods was entirely satisfactory, and many didn't work at all. Then, in the spring of 1999, I received an e-mail from Jerome Jenkins, a young chemist in St. Louis, Missouri, who was running a custom necktie company with his wife. He said he had a formula that chemically bonded printer-ink molecules to fiber molecules – the same way fiber-reactive dyes work. I was skeptical, but I sent for a sample of his formula. To my delight, it actually worked. Suddenly, everything was possible, and I spent the rest of 1999 experimenting with this wonderful elixir called Bubble Jet Set.

This is what we have all been waiting for – a magic formula that allows us to print color images directly onto fabric, at home, on our own inkjet printers. Bubble

RIGHT: Fabric printed from scanned leaves

Jet Set is a liquid fabric soak that makes inkjet and bubble-jet ink permanent and wash- able on 100 percent cotton and 100 percent silk. It leaves the fabric soft, as though it had been dyed, not crusty like painted fabric or "plas- ticky" like transfer paper images.

This book will help you start printing your own images onto fabric from scanned or copied photographs as well as every- day objects. I will give you tips and tricks for getting the best results and show you ways to use your computer to enhance your images. Don't worry if you're not computer savvy. I'll start by showing you how you can have a really good time using an inexpensive, all-in-one, printer- scanner-copier without even connect- ing it to a computer.

LEFT: Detail, CHRISTINE'S GARDEN, by the author. Full quilt pictured on pages 88–89.

The information in this book is based on my own experiences with printing on fabric as well as recommendations from the manufacturers of Bubble Jet Set and other fabric-printing products. Your own results will vary from one piece of fabric to the next and from one image to the next. Be prepared to have some fun experimenting with your printer and your fabrics to get the best results.

The most economical way to get printable fabric is to make your own treated fabric sheets, so we'll start with that in chapter 1. In the chapters that follow, you will see how to use your all-in-one printer to print directly onto fabric by copying photographs, along with everything but the kitchen sink (unless you can find one that fits on your copier bed). Then I will show you how to use your computer to edit your images and, finally, how to do "virtual appliqué" to combine images like the ones in STARS OF AFRICA on the cover of this book.

RIGHT: *Detail, CENTENNIAL, by the author. Full quilt pictured on pages 106–107.*

100

AND STILL GOING

Stars of Africa, 78" x 78", by the author

In 2000, I spent seven weeks touring and teaching in South Africa. This quilt grew out of the 43 rolls of film I took while I was there. The images I used were selected to illustrate the diversity, beauty, hope, and complexity of South Africa.

Using a technique I call "virtual appliqué," I used two or more photos to create each

of the diamond collages. Six diamonds come together to form kaleidoscopic images in the form of six-pointed stars. Between the stars I used individual diamond shapes that feature single animals and birds of South Africa. The lacy black border surrounding each of these diamonds was created from the silhouette of a typical flat-topped African tree.

Chapter One

GETTING READY TO PRINT ON FABRIC

Here's a how-to primer on using Bubble Jet Set and Bubble Jet Rinse to make inkjet images printed on fabric permanent and washable. As you begin to explore the fun you can have printing on fabric, remember to return to this chapter for tips and instructions on getting the best results with the process.

What You Will Need

- Natural-fiber fabric
- Freezer paper
- Plastic container
- Rubber gloves
- Bubble Jet Set
- Bubble Jet Rinse
- Inkjet printer

Use Bubble Jet Set and Bubble Jet Rinse to make images printed on fabric permanent and washable.

Bubble Jet Set 2000

This clear liquid soak is the secret for success in printing on fabric. It causes water-soluble inkjet ink to become insoluble and to bond permanently to treated fabric.

Bubble Jet Rinse

After printing, use Bubble Jet Rinse to remove the Bubble Jet Set chemical and any loose ink particles that have not bonded to the fabric.

Fabric

The manufacturer recommends 100 percent cotton or 100 percent silk because they give consistently reliable results. You can also print on linen, rayon, and acetate. On pages 82–83 (How Fabric Affects Print Quality), you will find more information on using different kinds of fabrics. As you will see, the results you get will be a little different with each fabric.

QUESTION
How much fabric will one bottle soak?

ANSWER

It depends on the absorbency and weight of the fabric. I generally use a fine, pima cotton broadcloth. One 32 oz. bottle of Bubble Jet Set will soak about seven yards, or 68 sheets precut to 9" x 11½". Muslin or heavy cotton sheeting will absorb more liquid. On the other hand, you may be able to soak 20 or more yards of lightweight silk with one bottle.

Freezer Paper

To run fabric through a printer, you need to stabilize it. You can use ordinary freezer paper from the grocery store. However, I like to use C. Jenkins Freezer Paper Sheets (see the resources list on page 118), which are precut to 8½" x 11", the width of a standard printer. The paper is slightly heavier than freezer paper, it resists rolling and curling, and it has a coating that adheres more easily to fabric than ordinary freezer paper. You can use the same sheet several times. After the first use, it is easier to get the sheets flat and free of air bubbles, and reusing the sheets brings the cost down to pennies per sheet.

Plastic Container

You will need a flat plastic container for soaking your fabric. The clear plastic storage containers sold in most hardware stores work well. Be sure your container is big enough for your fabric to lie flat in the bottom, but small enough for the Bubble Jet Set to cover the fabric without using too much of the liquid.

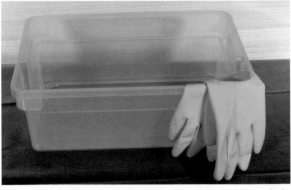

Use a container just big enough for the fabric to lie flat.

Rubber Gloves

As recommended by the manufacturer's safety precautions, always use rubber gloves when handling Bubble Jet Set, Bubble Jet Rinse, or any chemicals.

Pretreated Fabrics

If you don't want to do all the work yourself, pretreated fabric sheets are available and ready to put into the printer right out of the package (see the resources list on pages 118–121). The sheets are precut to 8½" x 11" and already bonded to a stabilizing paper. These chemically treated sheets save preparation time and provide a nice way to jump right into printing on fabric. Each brand of prepared sheets has specific instructions for use. Be sure to read the directions before you begin.

Inkjet Printer

You will need an inkjet printer. Any brand will work; the only exception is a small group of HP printers that use #10 and #11 ink cartridges. These printers are used primarily in businesses, but check to be sure that your printer does *not* use these two cartridges. If you are in the market for a new inkjet printer, the choices can seem daunting. Over time, I have used different models with a variety of features. The printer I used on the Simply Quilts show was a Hewlett-Packard (HP) model that scans, faxes, prints, copies, reads digital camera cards, and probably even cooks breakfast.

My current favorite printer is a more recent HP model with similar features. By the time you read this book, there will be newer models still. The good news is that in the years since Bubble Jet Set came on the market, the quality of inkjet printing has increased noticeably, while the time it takes to make a print and the prices of the printers have decreased.

Inkjet printers come in two varieties: single function (all they do is print) and multifunction (they do everything but walk the dog). Get one with the features you know you will use. A multifunction printer that includes a flatbed scanner will open a world of possibilities. You can scan or copy photographs or create your own fabric prints (like the ones on pages 112–113) from real objects without even hooking it to a computer (see chapter 2). Multifunction inkjet printer-scanner-copiers are available for $100 to $300

A multifunction printer-scanner-copier opens a world of possibilities for creating your own printed fabrics.

depending on added features, such as camera card readers, faxes, and picture-viewing screens. If you are interested in making larger images, there are printers available starting at around $300 that will allow you to print on fabric sheets as large as 13" wide by 50" long.

Using Bubble Jet Set

Follow these simple steps to make your own printable fabric sheets.

Step One:
Soak your fabric in Bubble Jet Set.

Cut your fabric into sheets slightly larger than the size you will be printing. For example, for a finished size of 8½" x 11", cut your sheets 9" x 11½". This allows for shrinking, and lets you trim the fabric to the exact size of a piece of copier paper with nice clean edges.

You can soak larger pieces of fabric folded, so they lie flat in your plastic container. I often cut my fabric into 50" lengths (the longest length my printer will print) and presoak several yards at a time. So when my Muse comes to visit, I have fabric ready to use.

To soak a whole stack of individually cut sheets, lay one sheet in the bottom of a flat plastic box and pour on enough Bubble Jet Set to saturate the fabric. Rub the liquid into the fabric until it is thoroughly soaked. Put a second sheet on top of the first so it can soak up the excess liquid. Pour a little more Bubble Jet Set on the second sheet and work it in.

Make sure the fabric is completely saturated with Bubble Jet Set.

Continue layering the fabric sheets one at a time, adding Bubble Jet Set each time and working it into the new sheet. This method will give you a stack of thoroughly soaked fabric with no excess liquid wasted in the bottom of the plastic container.

Note: If you fold and soak large pieces of fabric, be sure the liquid has penetrated through all of the layers.

A Word From the Manufacturer on Using Bubble Jet Set

Safety First
The manufacturer recommends that you use rubber gloves and work in a well-ventilated area. Please take these precautions to heart.

Manufacturer's Instructions
Here are recommendations from the manufacturer: Shake well and pour solution into flat pan. Saturate fabric in the solution for five minutes. Allow fabric to dry. Iron fabric to the smooth side of freezer paper. Cut size to fit your printer. Print on treated fabric, and let sit for 30 minutes. Wash in cold water with a mild detergent. For best results, wash with Bubble Jet Rinse. Use only as directed. Results may vary with different printers, inks, and fabrics.

Advice from the Manufacturer
In a newsletter to distributors and crafters using Bubble Jet Set, Jerome Jenkins had the following advice:

- This product cannot be made permanent with heat. If you attempt to heat set this product, it will have no effect whatever. The final step (washing the fabric with a mild detergent) is necessary to make Bubble Jet Set work correctly.
- This product only works with 100 percent natural fibers. If you use fabrics with synthetic blends, it will not work.
- Results will vary with different printers and different inks.
- Do not wash in cold water alone. You must also use a mild detergent when washing the fabric. Bubble Jet Rinse is recommended. If you do not wash in a detergent, it may bleed.
- Cold water alone will not remove all of the loose ink or remaining chemical from the fabric.
- Most important, please follow the instructions on the bottle.

Let the fabric soak for five minutes. Don't wring the fabric. The manufacturer recommends laying the soaked fabric on a towel so the Bubble Jet Set dries evenly through the fabric. I often hang it on the clothesline by the selvage edge with clothespins to dry. Do not drape the fabric over a bar or clothesline, because this will cause uneven distribution of the chemical through the fabric. If you hang the fabric outside, the manufacturer recommends keeping it out of direct sunlight.

Drying in the shade on a traditional clothesline with clothespins works nicely.

Prewashing fabric. It can't hurt to prewash your fabric before treating it with Bubble Jet Set, but this is not guaranteed to remove any finishes or sizing that may have been applied to the fabric during manufacturing. In the tests I have done, fabric finishes have not made a difference in the final image. However, because fabric comes from hundreds of different sources, it is not possible to know what finishes have been applied to your fabric. It is always a good idea to do a test print on each fabric you use before printing multiple images.

Storing pretreated fabric. The manufacturer recommends using treated fabric right away. The product reacts with oxygen, so the longer it sits, the more likely it is that it will react and no longer work. Personally, I have used fabric that was treated several months earlier, and it has worked fine. However, the fabric was stored inside an airtight plastic bag in a cool dry place. Before doing a big job, do a test print on fabric that has been sitting for any length of time to be sure it is still good.

QUESTION

Can I use something other than freezer paper to stabilize my fabric?

ANSWER

You can adhere your fabric sheets to copier paper or card stock with one of the repositionable aerosol adhesives on the market. There are many different brands, and all may not work equally well. I have had very good results with 3M Photo-Mount. Some of the embroidery and basting sprays available at quilt shops may work well. You can also use 8½" x 11" full-sheet-size self-adhesive labels, available in office supply stores.

Step Two:
Stabilize your fabric with freezer paper.
Freezer paper gives fabric enough stability to run through your printer. Place freezer paper, shiny side down, on top of your soaked and dried fabric.

With a dry iron, iron the freezer paper to the fabric. Turn the sheet over and iron again from the fabric side. Make sure there aren't any air bubbles between the fabric and the freezer paper. Air bubbles or loose areas along the edge of the fabric sheet can cause your print to smudge.

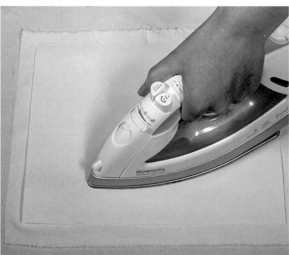

Start with a fabric sheet that is slightly larger than the freezer paper.

Note: Every iron is different. Adjust the heat setting on your iron to hot, but not hot enough to scorch your fabric.

After adhering your fabric to a stabilizer, cut the fabric to the width of your printer with a sharp rotary cutter. Be sure to check for little threads hanging off the edge of the fabric that might jam the printer head. Trim them off with a pair of sharp scissors.

Remove any loose threads with scissors.

If you are having trouble with the corners catching in your printer, it sometimes helps to cut a tiny triangle off the corners on each side of the leading edge.

To reduce curl, trim the corners off the leading edge.

For another way to reduce curl, iron a 1" wide strip of extra freezer paper to the leading edge. Position the shiny side of the strip against the paper side of the original freezer-paper sheet before ironing. Now your fabric is ready for your printer.

Cut a 1" wide strip of freezer paper.

Iron an extra strip of freezer paper to the leading edge to reduce curl.

Step Three:
Print on fabric.

These general instructions apply to most printers, but it wouldn't hurt to review the owner's manual for tips on how to use your printer and cautions on how to avoid paper jams or other actions that could damage your printer.

Before you put your fabric in the printer, check closely and remove loose threads and lint. If you print over a loose thread lying on the surface of your fabric sheet, it will leave a white, thread-shaped area on your image. The same is true of any loose slubs that may occur naturally in the weave of your fabric.

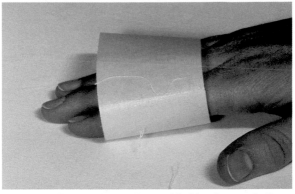

Remove loose threads and lint before printing.

A loose thread left on the fabric sheet leaves a white mark on the image.

Remove the paper from your printer's paper tray and load one sheet of fabric at a time in the tray.

Which side up? Make sure you know which side will be printed. Here's a simple test to find out which way to put your fabric in the paper tray. Mark a big "X" on a sheet of regular printer paper. Place the paper in the paper tray face up and print a very small image to save ink. If the image comes out on the side without the X, load the fabric into the tray fabric-side down. If the image comes out on the side with the X, load tray fabric-side up.

Loading the paper tray. If your fabric sheets are curling and making it difficult to load your paper tray, make a sandwich of two pieces of card stock with your fabric sheet in the middle. Use this sandwich to help slide your fabric sheet into the paper tray and align it correctly. Be sure to remove the top piece of card stock before printing.

Use card stock to help position curling fabric sheets in the paper tray.

On some printers, you can remove the catch tray to load the paper tray. If your fabric sheet is bowing up, you can leave the catch tray off after you have positioned your fabric in the paper tray, then you can very lightly hold the sheet flat just until the paper feed grabs the fabric.

Step Four:
After printing, rinse.

After putting your fabric through the printer, peel off the freezer paper, let the fabric sit for 30 minutes or more, then wash it in Bubble Jet Rinse.

Bubble Jet Rinse is designed to further set the ink that has reacted with your fabric and to remove any loose ink particles that haven't reacted. It takes at least two minutes for this rinse to be effective. Use *cold* water and keep the fabric moving for the full two minutes. Taking care with this step will prevent colors from bleeding.

The manufacturer recommends washing fabric sheets by hand because some washing machines can beat up and twist smaller swatches of fabric. Personally, I often put my printed sheets in the washer, but I always do a hand rinse first. If you just throw your printed fabric into the washer without the initial rinse, the fabric can fold back on itself while

QUESTION

I pretreated my fabric with Bubble Jet Set, but my images are not as brilliant as I had hoped they would be.

ANSWER

Bubble Jet Set is designed to make the images you print permanent. It won't improve the image that you started with, and it won't improve the performance of your printer. Printing on fabric is like printing on plain copier paper. The image will not be as brilliant as it looks on the computer screen or as sharp as it would be on expensive high-gloss photo paper. In chapter 3, you will find ways to enhance your images and get sharper, brighter, and more brilliant prints.

there are still loose ink particles on it. These particles can end up in the fold line or in other places on the fabric where you don't want them.

Drag each fabric sheet through the rinse solution to remove loose ink.

To hand rinse, use a capful or more of Bubble Jet Rinse to a basin with two or three gallons of water. Work with only one sheet at a time. Hold the fabric by two corners to prevent folding, and drag it back and forth through the solution for two minutes to remove as much loose ink as possible.

If you choose to do a machine wash, put four capfuls of Bubble Jet Rinse into the washer and set the water temperature for a cold wash and a cold rinse.

To dry the printed sheets, I usually put them in the dryer with an old towel to make them tumble better. The manufacturer recommends laying the sheets on a towel to dry or using a hair dryer on them if you're in a hurry.

Don't heat set printed fabric. Neither steam heat nor dry heat will have any effect as far as setting regular inkjet printer ink. In fact, if your iron dribbles, loose ink molecules can spread, causing water spots.

QUESTION
Can I use Synthrapol to remove loose dyes?

ANSWER
Yes, however, it is not the best choice. Synthrapol is designed to work chemically with fiber-reactive dyes, and Bubble Jet Rinse is designed to work with Bubble Jet Set and inkjet printer ink. Bubble Jet Rinse will actually further set the ink that has reacted with your fabric.

Chapter Two

COPYING IMAGES
ONTO FABRIC

The easiest way to print an image onto fabric is to set your all-in-one printer to Copy. Place the photo on the printer's glass and press Start. You don't even have to turn on your computer. The possibilities of having fun with copying are endless.

Getting to Know
Your Printer-Copier

Most all-in-one printer-copiers have essentially the same functions, which you operate from a control panel on the front of your machine.

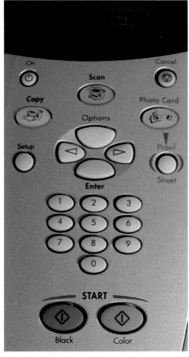

The function buttons on the control panel of your printer-copier will be similar to the ones on this HP all-in-one printer-scanner-copier.

QUESTION

What's the difference between copying and scanning when I print on fabric?

ANSWER

When you copy an image, it is sent directly to the printer. A scanned image is sent to your computer, where you can save the image and make a number of changes to it.

For copying, your machine will most likely have an Options button for selecting functions, such as Reduce/Enlarge or Lighter/Darker. As a rule, pressing the Options button repeatedly will cycle through the available copying functions. When you get to the option you want, pressing the Right/Left arrows (or Up/Down arrows on some printers) will cycle the printer through the settings for that function. For example, you can choose to enlarge a small photo to fit a full 8½" x 11" sheet. Pressing the Enter button confirms your selection. Note that most printers will switch back to the default settings after a few minutes.

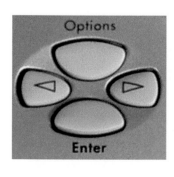

Your printer-copier will have function buttons for setting your copying preferences.

Many of today's printers give you a choice between printing black-and-white or color copies. Under the word Start, you will find Black for black-and-white copies and Color for making color copies.

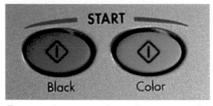

For color copies, be sure to press the Start Color button.

Copying Photos onto Fabric

To copy an image onto fabric, you place a photograph or some other object on the glass of your all-in-one printer, load the paper tray with a treated fabric sheet, and press one of the Start buttons.

QUESTION

Do I need to be concerned with copyright when printing images on fabric?

ANSWER

Absolutely. Everyone needs to be aware of copyright, and respect the intellectual property of others. Copying something for personal, non-commercial use is OK. Showing, selling, or otherwise profiting from someone else's image is not. Permission is needed if photos or images created by others are used. Personally I like to create my own images using objects from nature or my own original photographs.

Enlarging Photos

Most printers provide a number of options for enlarging or reducing photos. You can set a specific size such as 5" x 7", or you can use a custom setting to reduce or enlarge a photo to a given percentage of the photo's original size. Any number below 100 percent reduces the image, and any number above 100 percent enlarges it. The setting you are likely to use most often is Fit to Page, which resizes any image you place on the printer's flatbed to fit onto an 8½" x 11" sheet. Fit to Page makes your image as large as possible on a letter-sized sheet without changing the proportions of the original image.

Most printers have a Fit to Page option.

When you copy a small wallet-sized photo, keep in mind that the more you enlarge it, the fuzzier it will get. In chapter 3, on scanning and editing images, you will learn how to use your software to eliminate some of this fuzziness.

Note: To check how a copy will look on fabric, it's a good idea to make a copy on plain uncoated copier paper first.

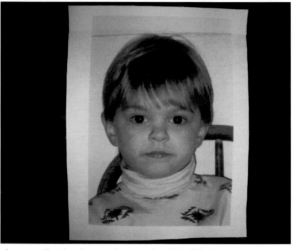

A small photo enlarged with Fit to Page may become fuzzier, but it may work fine for your quilt.

Enhancing Your Copies

The newer all-in-one printers provide some options for improving your color copies. These adjustments are often more effective if you scan your photos to your computer (see chapter 3). You may want to play with some of the settings when you are copying to see if your prints look better. You will probably find that the Default settings will give you the best results.

Original image of delphiniums

Using Fit to Page, this is a comparison of the normal (default) and best setting. There is very little difference in the printed fabric.

Using Fit to Page, this is a comparison of normal (default) and a darkening function. The printed fabric loses detail when darkened.

Copying Three-Dimensional Objects

Now, let's really have some fun. Look around your sewing room and see what you can find. Pile some leftover scraps from a quilt project on the glass and just hit the Start/Color button to create your own, original, one-of-a-kind fabric.

Copy scraps to create a unique fabric design.

Try placing objects on the glass and copying them with the lid open. Then try covering the objects with fabric for a different background effect.

Place the object on the glass.

Copying an object with the lid open gives you a black background.

Cover the object with fabric.

Print out your one-of-a-kind floral design.

Try copying everyday objects. See below and page 46 for some ideas. Anything goes. Just be careful not to scratch the glass on your copier when you place hard objects on it.

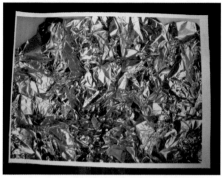

Wrinkled metallic wrapping paper

Gift bows

From my sewing room

Fresh fruit

Sprig of winter cherries

Scissors

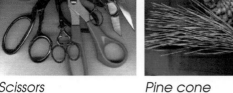
Pine cone

CD collection

QUESTION

My printer has an "A4" paper size listed in centimeters. Is this the same as regular letter-sized paper?

ANSWER

No. There are two standard paper sizes: 8½" x 11" letter size, used primarily in North America, and A4, a slightly narrower and longer international paper size used everywhere else.

Getting Special Effects

If you watch the action of the light bar as your printer is "reading" an object to be copied, you'll notice that it stops moving about every inch or so. If you move your picture or object across the strip of light every time the light bar moves, you can create wonderful abstract designs, and every design will be unique.

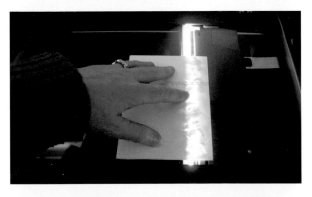

Sweep picture or object over the light, changing directions each time the bar moves.

Create a unique fabric collection from multiple special-effects copies.

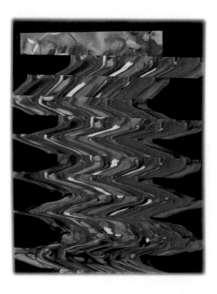

Swiping the light bar while you scan makes the image wavy.

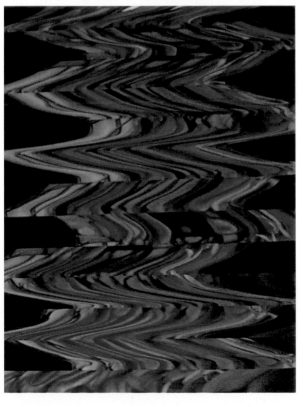

Use your imagination. The simplest objects become the basis of stunning one-of-a-kind images. In no time you will find you have created extraordinary designs.

Special effects from sweeping a single CD

CAUTION!

BE CAREFUL NOT TO SCRATCH THE GLASS. IF YOU ARE COPYING HARD OR SHARP OBJECTS, CONSIDER PLACING A SHEET OF CLEAR ACETATE OVER THE GLASS TO PROTECT IT.

Special effects from moving fabric scraps

SPLENDOR IN THE GRASS, 54" x 54", by the author

While our neighbors spread herbicide on their lawns in the spring, I take great delight in the cheerful and ubiquitous dandelion. Since 1999, when inkjet printing on fabric became possible, I haven't been able to resist the temptation to make an annual tribute to this persistent perennial.

I scanned the dandelion blossoms and leaves on a flatbed scanner, laying the blossoms directly on the glass and covering them with a piece of blue fabric. I designed the entire quilt in CorelDRAW® and used the Fibonacci sequence (1, 2, 3, 5, 8, 13, etc.) to determine the dimensions of the squares and rectangles.

Chapter Three

SCANNING AND EDITING IMAGES

Copying photos is the easiest and fastest way to print them onto fabric; however, if you want to make changes to your photos before you print them, you will need to scan your photos into the computer for editing. Get ready to have some fun!

Most printer-scanners and their software have essentially the same features as the all-in-one HP machine used for this chapter. Take a minute to familiarize yourself with the scanner functions of your machine, and be sure to read its user's manual so you can get the most out of the software.

Scanning Photos and Objects

To scan a photo or an object, place it on the glass and open your printer's software. Virtually all of the programs give you the option of previewing your image before scanning it. This is a nice feature when you are scanning a group of objects, because it lets you reposition things on the scanner bed before doing the actual print.

With a scanner, you have the option of resizing and setting the resolution either before or after scanning your photo. It's better to resize your photo before scanning. You can also make color and contrast adjustments before or after scanning, but you may prefer to wait for these until after scanning. When you're satisfied with the previewed image, start the scan.

QUESTION
What are the advantages of scanning vs. copying?

ANSWER
First of all, scanning allows you to save an image and use it later, or print multiple copies of the same image. It also allows you to preview the arrangement of three-dimensional objects on your scanner glass before committing them to fabric.

Saving an image to your computer allows you to do a number of things that you cannot do with copying alone. In addition to resizing, rotating, cropping, and changing the proportions of an image, you can change the image resolution, and improve the image with color and contrast adjustments. After your image is scanned you can make it larger than the width of your printer (see Piecing Oversized Images on pages 63–66). Images can be combined using "virtual appliqué" (see chapter 4) and you can have fun with the special effects available in paint programs. Finally, if you move objects during scanning to make custom fabric designs like the ones on pages 48–49, the image will be smoother, and you can save it to use again.

Resizing an Image

Image resolution goes hand in hand with resizing, so let's talk about that first. The resolution of an image is measured by the number of pixels per inch in a bitmap image. Every photograph and scanned image that you view on a computer is a bitmap made up of rows of tiny squares, called pixels. They blend to make an image, like a miniature postage-stamp quilt. The pixels in the figure below blend to make the area outlined in the child's photograph shown at the bottom.

Pixels in this bitmap image blend to make the outlined area (child's eye) in the figure below.

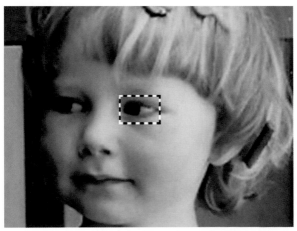

The pixels in the outlined area are shown enlarged in the figure above. Photo by Richard Howell.

The clarity of an image is determined by the resolution, also known as dpi, which is dots (that is, pixels) per inch. Images printed on fabric usually look best when printed at 200 dpi. If you plan to enlarge the image, it is best to use the resizing option in the scanner program before scanning, especially if you're enlarging a small wallet-sized photo to fit the page. Using this option will maintain the resolution and the clarity of the image as it is scanned. Enlarging a small image after scanning reduces the resolution and may result in a fuzzy image.

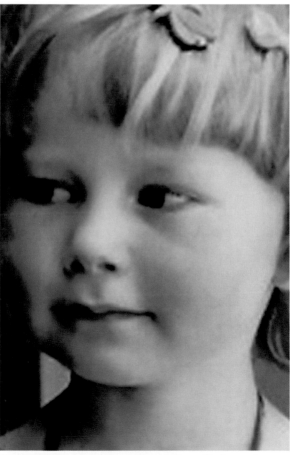

Enlarging an image after it has been scanned produces a bitmap with a lower resolution and loss of clarity.

To resize an image, set the width and height you want. The only limit to the width you select is the width of your printer carriage (most printers allow a maximum width of 8½").

Different brands of printers allow for a variety of height settings greater than 11", anywhere from 14" to 50". Simple scanner software usually does not allow for printing images larger than legal size. For larger images, you need to use a professional graphics program, such as CorelDRAW, Canvas™, Adobe® Photoshop, or Macromedia FreeHand. My favorite is CorelDRAW. Refer to Piecing Oversized Images on pages 63–66 to learn how to print and piece images that are larger than your printer will allow.

Your software will give you the option of keeping the same proportions as the original image when you enlarge it. However, if you choose not to keep the original proportions, you can have some fun setting different widths and heights to distort the image.

Set the resolution before starting the scan. It may be tempting to set a high resolution in the hopes of getting a sharper image on your fabric. For fabric printing, a resolution of 200 dpi is the highest you need to go. The weave of the fabric is seldom more than 200 threads per inch, so there is no point in printing at a higher resolution. At higher resolutions, the images use up a huge amount of memory and hard-drive space.

The original photo was 2" x 2".

Before scanning, the size was set at 3" x 3". Note that the proportions are the same as in the previous figure.

The proportions were intentionally not maintained so the image could be distorted.

Before printing your resized image, it is a good idea to do a couple of test prints on plain paper to see what you like the best. When the larger image is printed, you may be able to see differences in line definition and sharpness. You may also find that, on fabric, a softer (lower dpi) image works just as well.

When the scanning is finished, your picture will automatically go to some kind of imaging gallery, which usually shows thumbnail versions of your pictures. See your user's manual for exactly how your software works.

From the gallery of thumbnails, you will be able to open your image in a photo-editing program or save it with a file name and location of your choice. The image-editing program will have options for cropping, rotating, and adjusting color and brightness, among other things. If you plan to use a vector-graphics program, such as CorelDRAW, "import" your image into a new document, where you will be able to perform the changes described in

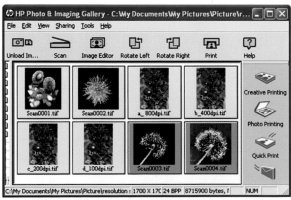

Thumbnails

this chapter. If you will be using a paint program, like Corel Photo-Paint®, just "open" the image file in that program.

Cropping Scanned Images

You can use a crop tool in your image-editing program to remove unwanted parts of a photograph. This tool works essentially the same way in most programs. See your user's manual to find out exactly how it works in yours.

In most imaging programs, the crop tool will resemble this one.

With the original scanned image open in your editing program, activate the crop tool (usually by just clicking on its icon), then drag a rectangle across the part of the photo that you want to keep. The parts of the photo outside the rectangle will be removed.

If you change your mind about how you want the photo cropped, before you complete the cropping action you can move the edges of the rectangle by dragging the little boxes in the sides and corners of the rectangle. Click OK to complete cropping your photo.

To crop images other than rectangles, or images with unusual shapes, you need a vector drawing program, such as Corel-DRAW (see the resources list on page 122).

View the original photo before it is cropped.

Preview the area you want to crop.

Adjust the rectangle for cropping.

Cropping removes unwanted parts of the original image.

Rotating Images

Depending on how you place the photo in your scanner, it may come out standing on its side. This can also happen when loading digital camera images taken with the camera held in a vertical position.

You can use the rotate function in your image-editing program to rotate the photo 90 degrees clockwise or counter-clockwise so it is right-side up. Many programs also provide the option of setting the angle of rotation yourself.

Piecing Oversized Images

You can create an oversized image on fabric by printing the image in strips the width of your printer carriage then sewing them together. To prepare the images, you need an image-editing software, such as CorelDRAW (see the resources list on page 122.)

1. For the best results, look for areas of the picture where there is pattern and contrast that will hide your seams. In theory, we could print this picture in two strips on a 13" wide-format printer. However, that would place the seam right down the middle of the baby's nose where it would show, so it was printed on three fabric strips, each 8½" wide and 25½" long.

2. Be sure to allow for some of the image to overlap. If you print the strips exactly the size needed for the finished image you will get white lines in places along the seam if you don't sew per-

fectly. With overlapping areas in the seam allowances, the image will look great even if your sewing isn't perfect.

Allow for the image to overlap between the strips.

Even if your printer has a "full bleed" feature, leave at least ¼" of white space when printing on fabric. Since fabric does not lie as flat as paper, printing all the way to the edge can cause your image to smudge.

3. Getting a perfect match when joining the strips is easy. Fold back and iron the seam allowance on one of the strips. Be sure to include part of the image in the seam allowance.

Fold back and press the seam allowance, making sure to include some of the image in the seam allowance.

4. Lay the fold along the edge of the next strip, and make sure everything in the image is perfectly aligned.

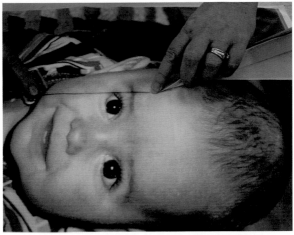

Align the image along the folded edge.

5. Run a little glue along the fold to hold everything in place. Then iron over the glued fold to set the glue.

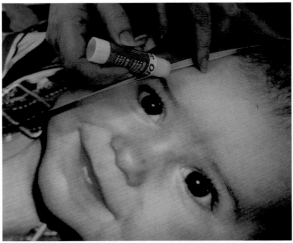

Glue and iron the folded seam allowance.

Note: Be sure to stitch the strips together before you wash them. Washing can cause shrinkage or distortion, making it more difficult to align the image.

6. Fold back the glued piece, so the right sides of your image are together, and stitch in the crease where the fabric was folded.

Stitch in the crease where the fabric was folded and pressed.

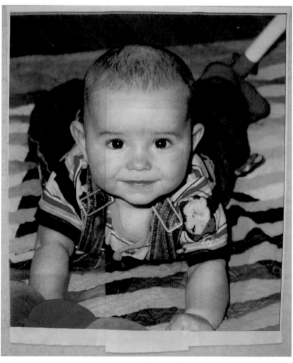

Oversized image, 22" x 25½", printed on three strips and pieced

A detailed tutorial on preparing larger images in CorelDRAW can be found under "Fabric Printing" at www.bryer-patch.com.

Scanning Three-Dimensional Objects

When you scan a photograph with the lid down on your scanner bed, the scanner reads the outline of the photo. The scan preview shows the entire scanner bed but outlines only what will be picked up in the scan.

The preview outline shows that only the photo will be scanned when the lid is closed.

On the other hand, when you scan three-dimensional objects, you have to leave the lid of the scanner partially open or all the way open. This results in the scanner reading more than just the object you have laid on the glass bed. In the photos on page 68, the shells in the corner of the scanner bed hold the lid partially open. The outlined area in the scan preview shows that the shells and the area of the glass not in contact with the lid will be scanned. Cropping the image and resizing it gives a nice close-up of the shells.

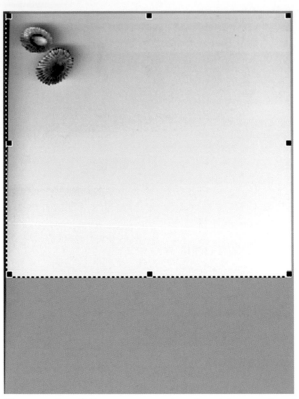

The parts of the scanner bed not in contact with the lid will be scanned.

Crop and resize the image to get a close-up of the shells.

Leaving the lid all the way open gives you a solid black background with the entire scanner bed included in the preview. All but the delicate dandelion seed head can be cropped from the scanned image.

Dandelion fluff scanned with the lid up

Scanned image resized and cropped

Scanning three-dimensional objects covered with fabric opens up a world of possibilities for creating backgrounds. I scanned a variety of dandelion blooms covered by blue fabric for the blocks in How Much Yellow Is Allowed, pictured on pages 116–117. The sashing strips are dandelion leaves scanned with the lid open, and the cornerstones are seed heads scanned with fabric behind them.

To protect a delicate bloom from the weight of a piece of fabric, place a cardstock ring around the bloom, then cover it with fabric, and preview the scan to check that the bloom is centered in the ring. Crop and resize the image to be printed onto fabric.

A cardstock ring cut from a file folder protects the fluff from the weight of the fabric.

The entire scanner bed will be included in the scan.

Cropping and resizing the scanned image creates a delicious close-up of the intricate dandelion fluff.

Getting the Best Images on Fabrics

Unlike copying, which sends an image straight to the printer, a scanned photo is sent to your computer. This gives you a chance to edit the photo before printing it. If you have a faded or dull photo, you can sometimes bring it to life by playing with color and contrast settings to improve how the image will look on fabric. As mentioned in chapter 1, the colors in a photograph printed on fabric are usually not as bright as they would be if they were printed on photographic paper. With the newest generation of printers, you will often find that you get the best results with the default settings on your printer and scanner. However, even with older equipment you can get more brilliant colors and sharper images by scanning and editing your pictures.

At the end of this chapter, I will show you some fun color effects you can get by pushing the boundaries of the color adjustments you can make. Most of the editing shown in this chapter can be done on the software that comes with your printer. However, you may get more predictable results by using the same functions in a professional drawing program or paint program, such as CorelDRAW, Adobe® Photoshop®, Corel Photo-Paint®, or Canvas™.

Fixing a Less Than Perfect Image

To get the best photographic images on fabric, you need to start with the best possible photographs. Printing on treated fabric will not improve your image or your photography. However, suppose you have an old family photo or a vacation shot, it's the only one you have, it's not great, but you just have to use it in your quilt. There are some adjustments you can make to photos before you print them that will help.

Virtually every photo-editing program has adjustments for contrast, the difference between lights and darks; saturation, the amount or purity of the colors; and hue, the names of the colors and where they fall on the color wheel or spectrum. Many programs also have an adjustment for brightness, or the amount of light in the photo. Different programs use different terms for these same functions.

The examples of color adjustments shown on page 75 are taken from the program that comes with one of the HP all-in-one printers. You will need to read your user's manual to learn what functions you have available in your pro-

QUESTION
What is the difference between a drawing program and a paint program?

ANSWER
Drawing programs are used for creating vector objects, which are described in more detail on page 96. Paint programs are used for editing pixels in bitmap images. Some drawing programs, such as CorelDRAW and Canvas™, have both vector-drawing and bitmap-editing features.

gram, what they are called, and how they work. The best way to learn these functions is to have some fun, play around with them, and see how they affect your photos.

Adjusting Contrast and Brightness

One of the functions I use the most is contrast. Your 4" x 6" photo may look great when you are holding it in your hand. However, when you enlarge it in your quilt and see it from six feet away, it may look dull. Adding contrast (increasing the difference between the lights and darks) may be the answer. In addition to increasing the contrast, decreasing the amount of light, or brightness, often helps bring out more detail.

The photograph on page 75, taken in 1903, has faded with time. By adding more contrast, we can restore many of the faded details and bring the picture back to life by making the darks darker and bringing out the white in the lighter areas. Next, decreasing the brightness brings back some of the detail in the white background.

There are no rules for setting these adjustments. With each photo, you need to experiment and see what gives you the best results. It's a good idea to test the prints on plain paper before committing them to fabric.

With the default contrast and brightness settings at 0, this old photo will fade even more on fabric.

Adding some contrast brings out details in the children, but washes out the back-ground.

Decreasing the brightness brings back some of the background detail.

Adjusting Color Saturation

You usually find the saturation adjustment under "color adjustment" or something similar. Saturation is the purity of your colors or the percentage of black they contain. Fully saturated colors contain no black. Increasing saturation will make your colors more intense and decreasing will take them closer to gray. In the following examples the center image (photo B) is the original. Decreasing the saturation to 0 percent removes the colors and turns them into shades of gray (photo A), and increasing the saturation to 100 percent maximizes the color intensity in photo C.

Combining Contrast and Saturation

When you combine an increase in contrast with an increase in saturation, you can get even more out of your photo. The photos of the lion on page 78 show how you can bring a photo to life by playing with the saturation and contrast adjustments. The original scanned lion in photo A is too dull to print well on fabric.

A.

B.

C.

Photo A shows what happens to the color in the original photo (B) when the color saturation is decreased to 0 percent. The bottom photo (C) shows what happens when the saturation is increased.

Increasing the saturation alone (photo B) does not get rid of the overall dullness of the photo. Increasing the contrast alone (photo C) doesn't bring out enough of the color. Combining an increase in both contrast and saturation (photo D) brings the photo to life for printing onto fabric.

Working with contrast and saturation: (a) original photo, (b) saturation alone increased, (c) contrast alone increased, (d) both saturation and contrast increased.

Starting with a Good Scanned Image

When you scan an object or a photo that looks fine the way it is, you may still need to slightly adjust the settings to get the same lively colors on fabric. Try increasing the saturation. Don't worry if the image looks a little garish on your monitor. It will tone down when it is printed on fabric.

Starting with a Good Digital Photo

If you use a digital camera and download your images directly to your computer, it may not be necessary to adjust the color settings at all. If your all-In-one printer has a camera-card slot, you can even print your images directly from your digital camera-card to your all-in-one printer without connecting to your computer.

You can download and print digital photos directly from your camera's memory card.

Even if a photo taken on a digital camera is a little dull, it can turn out just right on fabric. The only way to know for sure how your photo will turn out is to make a test print.

Original photo taken on a digital camera

The same photo printed onto fabric with no color adjustments

Adjusting Color Balance and Hue

Adjusting the color "balance" basically pushes every color in your picture toward a selected point on the color wheel. It's almost like covering your picture with colored cellophane. If the overall color of a photo is a little off as far as matching with other fabrics or photos in your quilt, you can push every color in the photo toward a different color family by adjusting the color balance.

ORIGINAL   RED   CYAN

MAGENTA   GREEN   YELLOW

BLUE

Changing the color balance in the first parrot image pushes all of the colors in the image toward the selected color.

Hue refers to the position where a color falls on the color wheel. A hue adjustment (the Color slider in HP Photo Editor) actually rotates every color in the picture an equal distance around the color wheel. The parrot's feathers in the original scanned photo are yellow. Five adjustments in hue give you five additional colorful parrots making up a fanciful color wheel or spectrum.

Changing the hue rotates each color in the image the same distance around the color wheel.

Starting with a Hopeless Photo

If you start with a photo that has little or no contrast, if the photo is out of focus, or if it is so dimly lit that you can't see any detail, no amount of tweaking on your computer will make the image printable. On the other hand, you may have a photo that's not great, but it has such sentimental value that you just have to use it in a quilt. By all means, fix it up the best you can, and use it.

How Fabric Affects Print Quality

In one of my earliest experiments, I printed the same 100 dpi image on as many different kinds of fabric as I could find in my studio and compared the results. The fabrics included pima cotton broadcloth, unbleached cotton muslin, bleached cotton print cloth, white silk satin, white silk charmeuse, white China silk, natural-colored silk broadcloth, white silk crepe de chine, and acetate satin.

Sharpness of image. Generally speaking, the higher the thread count, the sharper the image. The satin-finish fabrics had sharper images than the plain-weave fabrics with a similar thread count. The two sharpest images were the pima cotton broadcloth and the acetate satin.

Color. In general, the whiter the original fabric, the brighter and truer the colors were in the prints. The black ink did not do as well on the silk fabrics. It tended to look charcoal gray rather than true black. Black looked best on the cotton fabrics. The colored inks looked similar on all of the white fabrics. Because the inks are transparent, the colors of the unbleached fabrics showed through and softened all of the printed colors.

Ink Penetration. One of the fun things that happened with the lightweight silk was that the ink soaked all the way through to the back of the fabric; I could imagine using the banner setting to print a long silk scarf. On the heavier cotton fabrics, the back of the fabric was much lighter than the front.

Dye-Based Printer Inks

Most inkjet printer inks are made from dyes. The newer the printer, the better the image and the less you will need to do to make the image brilliant. Only a few years ago, printing on fabric with a top-of-the-line photographic printer resulted in faded, dull images, and major editing was required to improve the results. My tests on the latest models of HP printers have revealed that, in most cases, the default settings on the printer will produce the best results on fabric, and little or no editing of the photographs will be needed.

Unfortunately, the newer inks come in cartridges that cannot be used in older printers. If printing on fabric is going to be a major passion for you, I recommend investing in an up-to-date printer (at a fraction of the cost of a sewing machine). The qualities of the printed images, as well as the lightfastness and longevity of the newer inks, have improved significantly.

Wilhelm Imaging Research conducts research on the stability and preservation of digital color photographs and publishes the results on their Web site at http://www.wilhelmresearch.com. You may want to read their latest reports before choosing a new printer. Please keep in mind that these longevity studies were conducted on paper, not fabric. There are many different kinds of fabric, and fabrics are treated with many different chemicals, so the results you get will be different with each fabric.

While the print quality of less expensive inks may or may not be as good as the name-brand inks, the studies found that, in every case, the longevity of generic inks was less than the more expensive name-brand inks.

Dye-based inks, which are the choice of the fabric industry, tend to give better aesthetic results because of their translucence and their non-dusting characteristics. They remain the choice for all inkjet printer manufacturers for the highest quality photo-image printing.

In testing on fabric, HP dye-based inks provided just slightly less light- and wash-fastness than a good commercial print fabric and considerably better wash-fastness and somewhat less lightfastness compared to Pigma® Pens on fabric.

Note: On my 13" wide HP printer, there is an ink volume setting. I find that increasing the setting to maximum often gives me the best results.

Pigment-Based Inks

A handful of Epson printers and large-format HP printers are designed to use pigment-based inks that have more light- and wash-fastness than dye-based inks. These so-called archival inks have advantages and disadvantages. The obvious advantage is their washability on untreated fabric. Another advantage of pigment-based ink is that you can print on synthetics. In my testing on synthetics, the color inks were washfast, but the black ink tended to wash out on some polyesters.

The disadvantage is that images printed on fabric are not as brilliant or sharp as images made with the more common dye-based inks. Printers and inks are improving all the time, so by the time you read this book, some of the pigment inks may give results that are as good as dye-based inks.

When I first tried pigment-based ink, I was concerned that it might crack or wear off like some of the old transfer images. I printed images as large as 13" x 44", and have carried them around in my suitcase as samples for several years, folding and unfolding them dozens of times. I have seen no deterioration of the images at all.

CHRISTINE'S GARDEN (pictured on pages 88–89) was printed on a 2000P model Epson with pigment-based ink. It hung for over a year, next to a window that got afternoon sun, and showed no signs of fading.

THE BOTTOM LINE ON FADING

While we can't predict exactly how long printed fabric will resist fading, we do know that UV rays fade all fabric, and the more UV your fabric is exposed to, the faster it will fade. If your printed quilts will be on display regularly, I recommend treating them with a protective spray like QuiltGard® Fabric Protector to delay fading as long as possible (see resources list on page 122).

Note: I do not recommend refilling cartridges. I tried it and found that I had no problem refilling them. They just didn't work afterward. Save your money.

CHRISTINE'S GARDEN, 49" x 41", by the author

This virtual appliqué quilt grew out of a series of photographs taken with a macro lens to get close-up details. I scanned the photos and imported them into Corel-DRAW, where I clipped and arranged them to make the final design. The rectangle with the large iris blossom floats over

a background made from a greatly enlarged photo of the inside of an iris. Clematis blossoms and vines form a border around the outside of the quilt. The inner green border is made from a photo of moss growing in a stream. All of the fabrics in this quilt were printed with archival inks.

DETAIL: *STARS OF AFRICA*, by the author.
Full quilt pictured on pages 16–17.

Chapter Four

VIRTUAL APPLIQUÉ

If you are computer savvy, you can get really creative with something I call "virtual appliqué." Instead of cutting fabric into irregular shapes and assembling them into an image, in virtual appliqué, you cut up and assemble parts of photographs or scanned images into a composite image on your computer, then print it onto fabric. To do this you need software like CorelDRAW, which has vector graphics (line drawing) and clipping features (see the resources list on page 122). In CorelDRAW, you can draw outlines in any shape you like. A feature called Power Clip lets you use the shapes to crop your photograph or scanned image. Imagine the shape as your template, and the image as your fabric. You can use other features of CorelDRAW to assemble your virtual appliqué pieces into a complete design before printing it on fabric.

Using Virtual Appliqué to Combine Photos

Let me show you a simple potholder project to introduce you to virtual appliqué. You will then be able to apply this same process to more complex designs, like CHRISTINE'S GARDEN (pages 88–89) or STARS OF AFRICA (pages 16–17).

Begin by scanning the photos for your appliqué into a vector graphics program.

Use virtual appliqué to embellish a snapshot.

Scan photos into a vector graphics program.

This project begins with two 4" x 6" snap-shots scanned into CorelDRAW. Because both photos looked good on the computer, they were scanned with the default settings on my scanner display screen. No contrast or saturation adjust-ments were made. If your image needs to be fine-tuned, this is the best time to do it, before you start to play. See chap-ter 3 for tips on fine-tuning your images.

For a virtual-appliqué flower, create a closed vector shape by outlining the flower and some leaves. Then use your software's clipping function to remove everything but the image inside the vector object. Make several copies of the flower shape.

Outline the flower and leaves with a vector object.

Clip to remove all but the appliqué piece.

Draw a square with rounded corners the size of a potholder. Your vector graphics program will have options for doing this easily. Place your portrait snapshot in the square and rotate it so it will be right side up when the potholder is hanging by one corner. You may also want to make the portrait a little larger or smaller to fit the proportions of the potholder.

Place and rotate the snapshot with the child's face in the center of the potholder outline.

Now you're ready to compose your potholder design. One at a time, place the flowers around the face. By rotating, mirror imaging, and resizing the flower, you can create the illusion of a wreath containing many different flowers (page 97).

When you have everything arranged to your liking, use your software's clipping function to contain the composite image within the potholder shape. Center the potholder on the page, and hit the print button. Do a print preview to make sure you will be printing what you really want to print.

These are essentially the same steps I used to create the individual diamonds in STARS OF AFRICA, pictured on pages 16–17.

Virtual Appliqué for the Technologically Clueless. If you are not computer savvy, you can still have fun with a project of this kind. Print the portrait snapshot and multiple copies of the flower on paper. Cut out the flowers with scissors and paste them together to frame the face. Then copy the whole composition onto fabric.

QUESTION
If I want to try virtual appliqué, should I start with something simpler than CorelDRAW?

ANSWER
Digital cameras and the simpler programs that come with scanners usually do not have clipping functions. This function used in virtual appliqué is found in professional vector-drawing programs, such as CorelDRAW. You will discover that the simpler programs are limited, whereas the possibilities with vector-drawing programs are limitless. On the other end of the spectrum, you have Adobe's very expensive and complex Photoshop® and Illustrator® programs. They both have the drawing and clipping functions, but they are much more difficult to learn. See the resources list on page 122 for more information on getting an affordable (under $80) version of CorelDRAW.

Create a flower wreath around the child's Face.

Assemble all your appliqué flowers under the outline of the shape, then use the potholder shape to clip the image.

QUESTION

What is the difference between a vector object and a bitmap?

ANSWER

Vector objects, also called Beziér curves in some software programs, are made up of straight and curved lines drawn on a computer. Bitmaps are images made up of rows of tiny squares called pixels. The small stars in the following figures look the same in their normal view. The enlarged views next to the stars show the pixels in the bitmap, while the vector object is still a line. When you do "virtual appliqué" you use vector objects to draw shapes for clipping your scanned bitmap images. Think of the vector object as your template, and the bitmap as your fabric.

A bitmap image shown in normal view (left) and in enlarged view (right)

A vector object shown in normal view (left) and in enlarged view (right)

You could even reuse the same frame for every member of your family.

Using Special Effects

"Paint" programs such as Photoshop, Corel Photo Paint, and a long list of others, are specifically designed for editing the individual pixels in your pictures. In each of these programs there are some special effects that go beyond normal contrast and color adjustments. These are lots of fun to play with, and have unlimited potential for new images on fabric. Let me give you one example of what I did with a 4 x 6 snapshot of a rose.

First, I scanned the photo, cropped it to make it square, and opened it in Corel Photo Paint. I spent less than half an hour playing with the functions under the word "effects" at the top of the screen, and made all of these fun variations. Virtually every professional paint program on the market has these same functions.

This is the same rose we used in the potholder project.

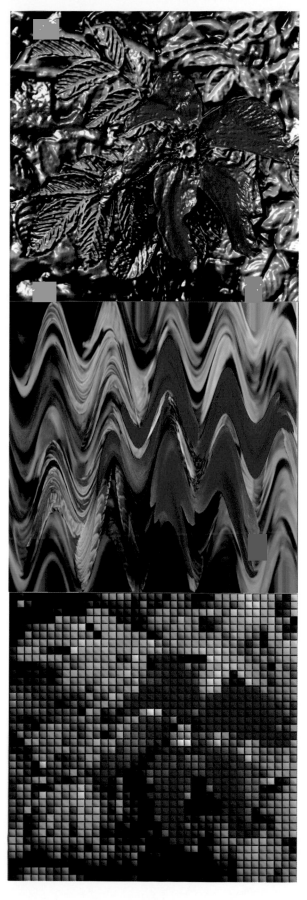

For the quilt CERTAIN POSSIBILITIES: DEATH, TAXES AND DANDELIONS (pictured on pages 108–109) I scanned a single real dandelion blossom, then applied every special effect I could find – and printed the ones I liked the best. I used my favorites on the front, and the leftovers on the back.

The wonderful thing about using special effects is that you don't have to know anything to get great results. Just click on a function, try it out, and see what you get. If you like it, print it on fabric, and if you don't like it, use my very favorite function – Undo.

The most important thing is to have fun playing.

Quilt back (above) and permutations of dandelions from Certain Possibilities: Death, Taxes and Dandelions, *by the author. Full quilt pictured on pages 108–109.*

I made this quilt in honor of my father, Cecil Joseph Bryer, who celebrated his 100th birthday on July 24, 2001. The hundred guests, who celebrated with him, included his three children, nine grandchildren, and 15 great-grandchildren. Dad lives in the house he bought in 1937. On his birthday he drove his car one last time, then donated it to charity – his one concession to being a centenarian.

Centennial #1, 22" x 18", by the author

The large photo was taken on his 100th birthday. The small photos surrounding his head trace his life from his baby picture in 1901 to his 99th birthday in 2000. The pictures were scanned into the computer, and the center panel of the quilt was designed in CorelDRAW then printed with archival ink on cotton broadcloth treated with Bubble Jet Set.

CERTAIN POSSIBILITIES: DEATH, TAXES AND DANDELIONS,
30" x 48", by the author

This quilt was made especially for the exhibition Oxymorons: Absurdly Logical Quilts! When I was asked to be in this exhibit, I chose the oxymoron "Certain Possibilities," thinking it would be fun to present a single image in many different ways. I chose the old axiom "The only thing certain is death and taxes." As I began working on this theme, I found it a bit dark and depressing. Then it occurred to me that dandelions must be at least as ubiquitous as taxes, so I decided to include them in my oxymoron quilt.

For the dandelions, I used a "paint" program to apply different special effects to the same scanned image of a dandelion. In the final quilt design, I used 15 variations of the original scanned dandelion, then used 16 more variations on the back of the quilt.

HIDDEN INFLUENCES #2, 36" x 41", by the author

Hidden Influences is a collage of photographs and graphics designed in CorelDRAW. The two faces float behind a field of rainbow colored checks. I printed this quilt in three 12" sections, then I sewed the strips together to form the complete image.

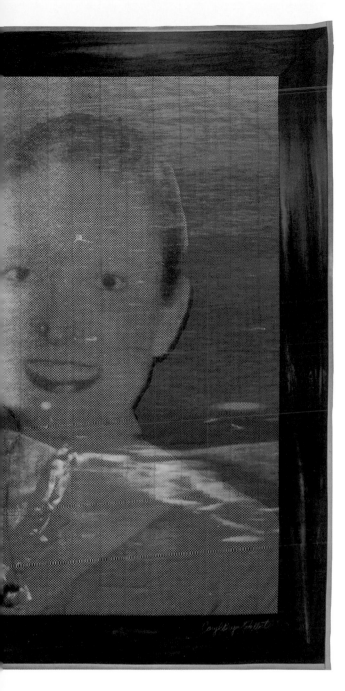

The photographs of my great-grandmother and me were taken approxi-
mately 100 years apart. My father, who
was born in 1901, still remembers his
grandmother as the kindest person he
ever met. Although I never met her, my
great-grandmother's influence can be
felt through her picture and through my
father's kind and gentle nature.

OSWEGO AUTUMN #1, 18" x 18", by the author

OSWEGO AUTUMN was made in the fall of 1999 as an experiment in creating my own fabrics from photos for a traditional block. The photos were taken in October when the colors in our little midwest-

ern town are at their most glorious. The leaves were photographed at different distances, and range from a close-up of the leaf veins to a distant picture of a tree branch.

KORUNDA, 18" x 18", by the author

Korunda, in Queensland, Australia, has a wonderful bird sanctuary where you can take pictures of the colorful native

birds of Australia at very close range. I used my own manipulated photos of parrots instead of commercially printed fabric to create this traditional block.

HOW MUCH YELLOW IS ALLOWED, 62" x 62",
by the author

This is the silliest quilt I made in 2000, but also the most fun. It began when I wondered what would happen if I scanned a dandelion directly on my flat bed scanner. By scanning at a very high resolution and then blowing up the dandelions, I discovered that every dandelion has its own personality. To scan the dandelions, I cut off the stems and laid them face

down on the glass of the scanner. I covered them with a piece of blue cloth.

I had so much fun with the flowers, I decided to make a whole quilt of dandelion images. The sashing strips are direct scans of dandelion greens, and the cornerstone blocks are additional scans of the blossom, gone to seed.

RESOURCES

Many local quilt shops carry the products mentioned in this book. Please support your local shops and buy these products there if they are available.

The product brand names listed in red are available online from the author at The Bryerpatch Studio Internet Store, www.bryerpatch.com.

Fabric Treatment:
Bubble Jet Set and Bubble Jet Rinse
(for making your own fabric sheets)
C.Jenkins Necktie & Chemical Co.
www.cjenkinscompany.com

Alternative kit for making fabric sheets:
Soft Fabric Photos
www.softfabricphotos.com

Freezer Paper Sheets:
C. Jenkins Freezer Paper Sheets
(both 8½" x 11" and 12" x 15" for larger projects)
C.Jenkins Necktie & Chemical Co.
www.cjenkinscompany.com

Pre-treated Fabric Sheets:
Miracle Fabric Sheets™
C.Jenkins Necktie & Chemical Co.
www.cjenkinscompany.com

Printed Treasures® (fabric sheets)
Milliken & Co.
www.milliken.com

Color Plus® Fabric Sheets
(custom, wide rolls of pretreated fabric and fabric sheets in silk, linen, and rayon)
Color Textiles Inc.
www.colortextiles.com

RIGHT: *Detail, BUBBLE JET SET
by the author*

Caryl Bryer Fallert

EQ Inkjet Fabric Sheets
The Electric Quilt Company
www.electricquilt.com

June Tailor Printer/copier fabrics and transfer papers
June Tailor
www.junetailor.com

Needles:
Schmetz Microtex Sharp 60/8 (recommended with fine thread and monofilament)
www.schmetzneedles.com

Print Permanence Data:
Wilhelm Imaging Research
www.wilhelm-research.com
(Print permanence data for all brands of printers)

Printers, Scanners, and Ink:
Hewlett Packard
www.hp.com

Epson
www.epson.com

Canon
www.canon.com

Service/Custom printing on fabric:
Custom printing on regular size printers
Soft Fabric Photos
www.softfabricphotos.com

Custom printing of very high quality images on wide format printers
Stork Digital Imaging
www.stork-digital-imaging.com

Software:

Quilt Labels:
HP custom quilt label kit
www.shopping.hp.com

Paint program and vector drawing program with "clipping" function bundled together:
Corel Graphics Suite 12
CorelDRAW Essentials 2 (older version of Corel which is more economical when you are just getting started.)
Corel Inc.
www.corel.com

Threads:

The Bottom Line™: Bobbin weight thread for joining seams in photos
MonoPoly: Invisible polyester thread for quilting on photos
Superior Threads
www.superiorthreads.com

UV Fabric Protector:

Quiltgard® Fabric Protector w/UV Sun Screen
The Craftgard Co.
www.craftgard.com

RIGHT: *Detail, SPLENDOR IN THE GRASS, by the author. Full quilt pictured on pages 52–53.*

Photo by Context Media

ABOUT THE AUTHOR

Caryl Bryer Fallert is internationally recognized for her award-winning art quilts. While her style of quilting is recognizable, her work is constantly evolving. When she first printed photos on fabric in 1999, it seemed that she had diverged from her usual style. Recently, however, her digital fabrics have found their way into the graphic curved piecing for which she is known. Caryl finds her greatest joy in designing and making her quilts and sharing what she has learned with students in her workshops and lectures, which have taken her to eleven countries on five continents.

In 2002, Caryl was selected as one of the 30 most influential quiltmakers in the world. She is the only three-time winner of the American Quilter's Society Best of Show Award, and her quilts have won Best of Show in more than fifteen other national and international exhibitions. Special Awards include the Bernina of America Quilt Leadership Award (2003), National Quilting Association Master-piece Quilt Award (1986), the International Quilt Association Master Award for Contemporary Artistry (2002), and Master Award for Machine Artistry (1997). Her quilt CORONA #2: SOLAR ECLIPSE was voted one of the 100 Best Quilts of the Twentieth Century.

Caryl's work has been exhibited around the world, and can be found in public, museum, corporate, and private collections in twenty-two states and seven foreign countries. Collections include: The Museum of Contemporary Arts and Design, Illinois State Museum, Rocky Mountain Quilt Museum, American Quilt Study Center, and the Museum of the American Quilter's Society.

Her quilts have appeared in hundreds of national and international publications, including the covers of two Quilt National Catalogs. Caryl publishes a series of workshops on CD-ROM, which are available at quilt shops and through her Bryerpatch Studio Internet store.

More information about Caryl, her quilts, patterns, CDs, and printing on fabric is available at:
http://www.bryerpatch.com

OTHER AQS BOOKS

This is only a small selection of the books available from the American Quilter's Society. AQS books are known worldwide for timely topics, clear writing, beautiful color photos, and accurate illustrations and patterns. The following books are available from your local bookseller, quilt shop, or public library:

QUILT SAVVY
Simple Thread Painting
NANCY PRINCE

#6519 $21.95

QUILT SAVVY
Hand Quilting
Virginia "Rusty" Hedrick

#6294 $21.95

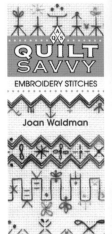

QUILT SAVVY
EMBROIDERY STITCHES
Joan Waldman

#6520 $21.95

QUILTERS *Playtime*
Games with Fabrics
Dianne S. Hire

#6295 $24.95

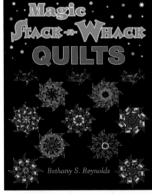

Magic STACK-n-WHACK QUILTS
Bethany S. Reynolds

#4995 $19.95

Keepsake SIGNATURE QUILTS
Sally Saulmon

#6208 $24.95

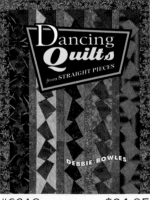

Dancing Quilts from STRAIGHT PIECES
DEBBIE BOWLES

#6210 $24.95

LOOK for these books nationally.

CALL **1-800-626-5420**

or VISIT our Web site at

WWW.AMERICANQUILTER.COM